PIANO

HYMNS
MAGNIFIED
15 EMBELLISHED ACCOMPANIMENTS

ARRANGED BY JAMES KOERTS

ISBN 978-1-4803-3868-5

Shawnee Press

EXCLUSIVELY DISTRIBUTED BY

HAL•LEONARD®
CORPORATION

7777 W. BLUEMOUND RD. P.O. BOX 13819 MILWAUKEE, WI 53213

In Australia Contact:
Hal Leonard Australia Pty. Ltd.
4 Lentara Court
Cheltenham, Victoria, 3192 Australia
Email: ausadmin@halleonard.com.au

Visit Shawnee Press Online at
www.shawneepress.com

Visit Hal Leonard Online at
www.halleonard.com

ALL HAIL THE POWER OF JESUS' NAME

Words by EDWARD PERRONET
Altered by JOHN RIPPON
Music by OLIVER HOLDEN

Hymnal Version

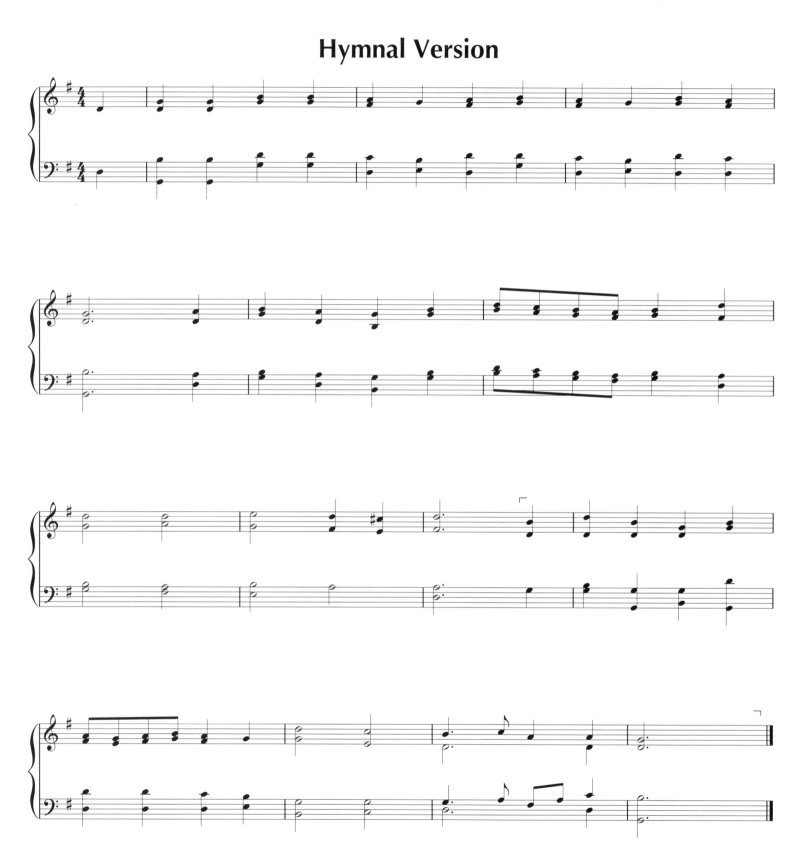

Alternate Accompaniment

Arranged by JAMES KOERTS

BE THOU MY VISION

TRADITIONAL IRISH
Translated by MARY E. BYRNE

Hymnal Version

Alternate Accompaniment

Arranged by JAMES KOERTS

THE CHURCH'S ONE FOUNDATION

Words by SAMUEL JOHN STONE
Music by SAMUEL SEBASTIAN WESLEY

Hymnal Version

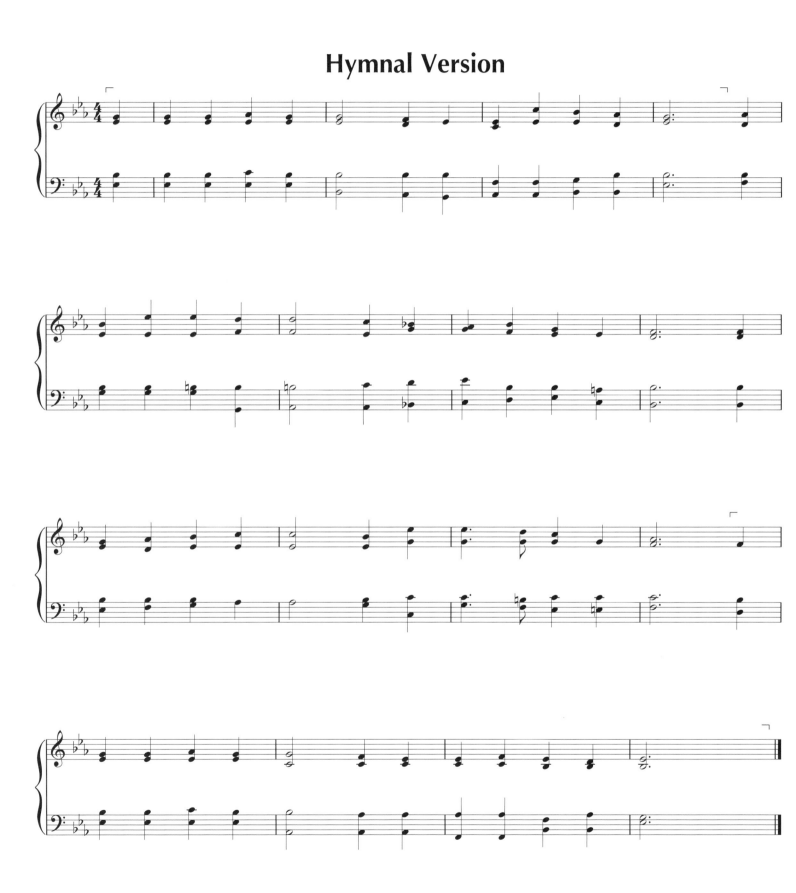

Alternate Accompaniment

Arranged by JAMES KOERTS

CROWN HIM WITH MANY CROWNS

Words by MATTHEW BRIDGES and GODFREY THRING
Music by GEORGE JOB ELVEY

Hymnal Version

Alternate Accompaniment

Arranged by JAMES KOERTS

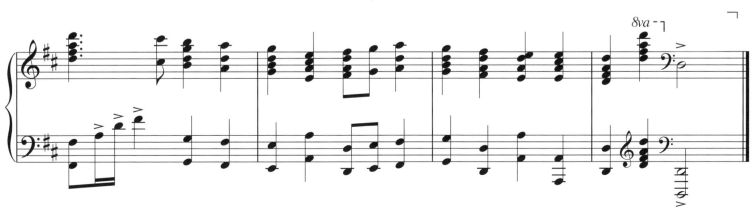

GRACE GREATER THAN OUR SIN

Words by DANIEL B. TOWNER
Music by JULIA H. JOHNSTON

Hymnal Version

Refrain

Alternate Accompaniment

Arranged by JAMES KOERTS

Refrain

HOLY, HOLY, HOLY

Text by REGINALD HEBER
Music by JOHN B. DYKES

Hymnal Version

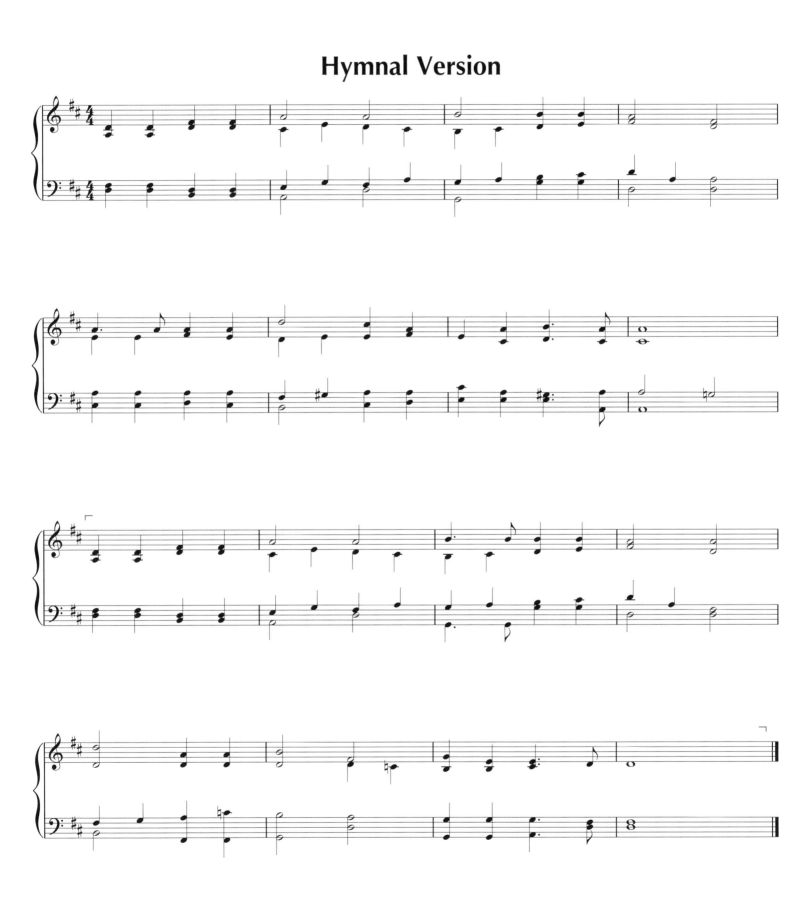

Alternate Accompaniment

Arranged by JAMES KOERTS

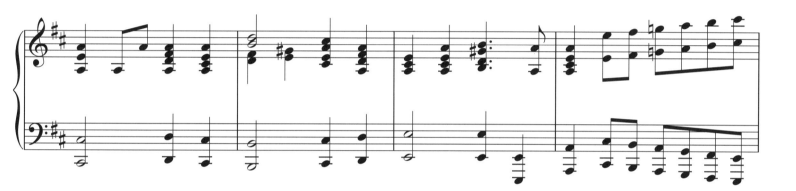

I LOVE TO TELL THE STORY

Words by A. CATHERINE HANKEY
Music by WILLIAM G. FISCHER

Hymnal Version

Refrain

Alternate Accompaniment

Arranged by JAMES KOERTS

Refrain

15

I NEED THEE EVERY HOUR

Words by ANNIE S. HAWKS
Music by ROBERT LOWRY

Hymnal Version

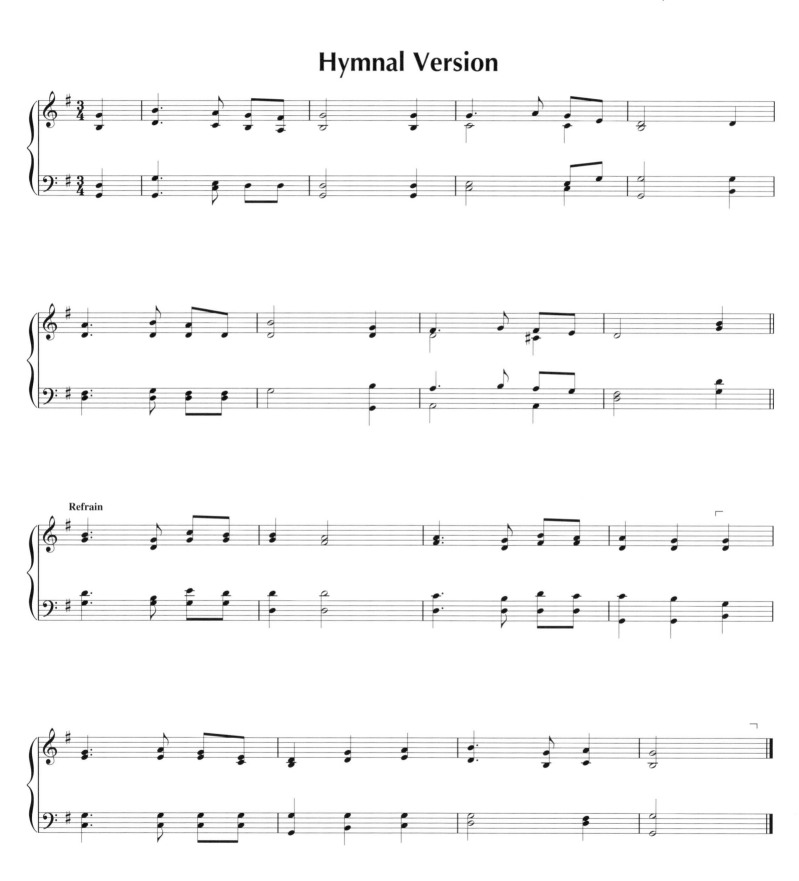

Alternate Accompaniment

Arranged by JAMES KOERTS

Refrain

I SING THE MIGHTY POWER OF GOD

Words by ISAAC WATTS
from *Gesangbuch der Herzogl*

Hymnal Version

Alternate Accompaniment

Arranged by JAMES KOERTS

IT IS WELL WITH MY SOUL

Words by HORATIO G. SPAFFORD
Music by PHILIP P. BLISS

Hymnal Version

Alternate Accompaniment

Arranged by JAMES KOERTS

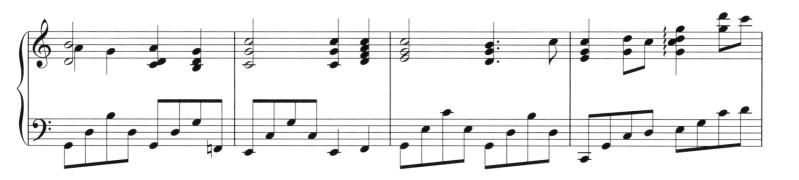

Refrain

LEANING ON THE EVERLASTING ARMS

Words by ELISHA A. HOFFMAN
Music by ANTHONY J. SHOWALTER

Hymnal Version

Alternate Accompaniment

Arranged by JAMES KOERTS

Refrain

A MIGHTY FORTRESS IS OUR GOD

Words and Music by MARTIN LUTHER
Translated by FREDERICK H. HEDGE
Based on Psalm 46

Hymnal Version

Alternate Accompaniment

Arranged by JAMES KOERTS

MY FAITH LOOKS UP TO THEE

Words by RAY PALMER
Music by LOWELL MASON

Hymnal Version

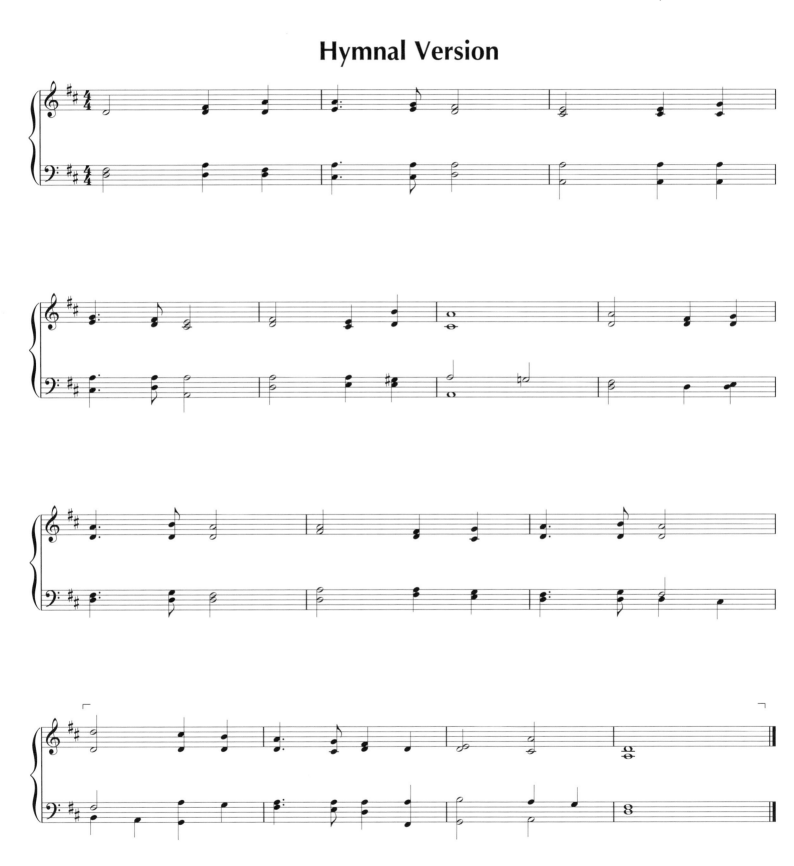

Alternate Accompaniment

Arranged by JAMES KOERTS

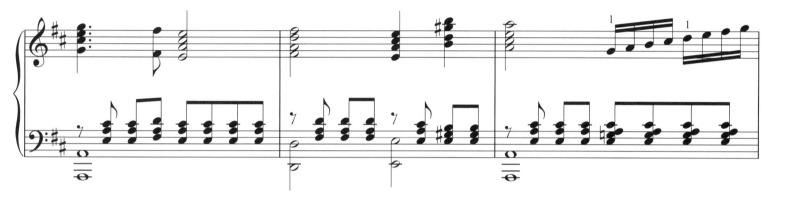

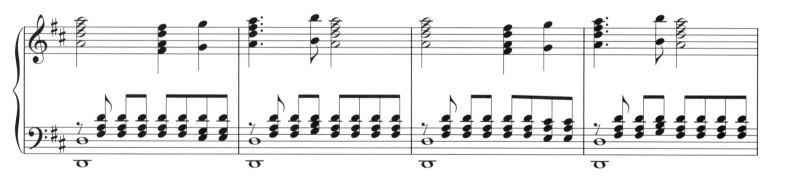

8vb

'TIS SO SWEET TO TRUST IN JESUS

Words by LOUISA M.R. STEAD
Music by WILLIAM J. KIRKPATRICK

Hymnal Version

Refrain

Alternate Accompaniment

Arranged by JAMES KOERTS

Refrain

WHAT A FRIEND WE HAVE IN JESUS

Words by JOSEPH M. SCRIVEN
Music by CHARLES C. CONVERSE

Hymnal Version

Alternate Accompaniment

Arranged by JAMES KOERTS

PIANO & ORGAN COLLECTIONS
from Shawnee Press

BEGINNING ORGANIST – VOLUME 1

by Darwin Wolford

Each piece is carefully edited, complete with fingerings and pedal indications, making it an excellent teaching resource. Includes: "Duet" by Handel, "From Heaven on High" by Reger, "Voluntary" by Boellmann, "Andante" by Zollner, and "In Dulci Jubilo" by Bach.

_____ 35001866 Organ Solo..............................$14.99

FIFTEEN PIECES FOR CHURCH OR RECITAL

by Gordon Young

Includes: Air • Antiphon • Bachiana • Benedictus • Canzona • Concertino • Divertissement • Glorificamus • Marche • Offertorium • Postludium • Prelude on "Blessed Assurance" • Toccata • Trumpet Gigue • Trumpet Voluntary.

_____ 35006677 Organ Solo..............................$19.99

GO OUT IN JOY – FESTIVE POSTLUDES FOR PIANO

A variety of styles and difficulty levels are included, with careful attention paid to choose hymns that have the spirit of celebration in both tune and text. Enjoy the work of Vicki Tucker Courtney, Cindy Berry, Brad Nix, Alex-Zsolt, Hojun Lee and others!

_____ 35028092 Piano Solo..............................$16.99

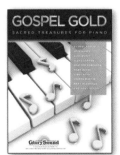

GOSPEL GOLD

Featuring Arrangements from: Cindy Berry, Patti Drennan, Mark Hayes, Lloyd Larson, and others

Some of today's best pianists and arrangers have gathered to celebrate the best timeless gospel hymns in a new compilation sure to be a hit with any church pianist. 17 songs, including: Stand Up, Stand Up for Jesus • 'Tis So Sweet to Trust in Jesus • Just a Closer Walk with Thee • Do Lord • Rock of Ages • He Keeps Me Singing • and many more.

_____ 35027306 Piano Solo..............................$16.99

GOSPEL GOLD – VOLUME 2

Stretch your offertory options with this brilliant collection from some of today's most respected piano arrangers: Mary McDonald, Pamela Robertson, Shirley Brendlinger, Brad Nix, James Koerts, Carolyn Hamlin and others.

_____ 35028093 Piano Solo..............................$16.99

HYMNS OF GRATEFUL PRAISE

arr. Lee Dengler

Includes: For the Beauty of the Earth • Joyful, Joyful We Adore Thee • Morning Has Broken • Fairest Lord Jesus • Now Thank We All Our God • Holy God We Praise Thy Name • All Creatures of Our God and King • Praise to the Lord the Almighty • Praise Him! Praise Him! • and more.

_____ 35028339 Piano Solo..............................$16.99

IMAGES

arr. Heather Sorenson

When combined with the innovative visual supplement, the church pianist moves their ministry from its traditional role into a new area of expression. Includes: Beautiful • I Surrender All • Fairest Lord Jesus • Blest Be the Tie • I Must Tell Jesus • It Is Well • Brethren We Have Met to Worship • Whiter Than Snow • A Mighty Fortress • The Journey (with He Leadeth Me).

_____ 35028265 Piano Solo..............................$16.99
_____ 35028266 Listening CD............................$16.99
_____ 35028277 Piano Solos Book/
DVD-ROM Pack.......................$29.99

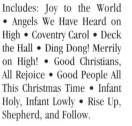

JOY TO THE WORLD

arr. Jack Jones

Includes: Joy to the World • Angels We Have Heard on High • Coventry Carol • Deck the Hall • Ding Dong! Merrily on High! • Good Christians, All Rejoice • Good People All This Christmas Time • Infant Holy, Infant Lowly • Rise Up, Shepherd, and Follow.

_____ 35028373 Organ Solo..............................$16.99

MUSIC OF THE MASTERS FOR THE MASTER

Using a classical theme or genre as the basis for each piece, the composer weds a time-honored hymn to bring these beloved themes into the sanctuary. Included in this thoughtful assembly is the writing of Mary McDonald, Cindy Berry, Carolyn Hamlin, Joseph Martin, Alex-Zsolt, Jack Jones, James Michael Stevens and many others.

_____ 35028091 Piano Solo..............................$19.99

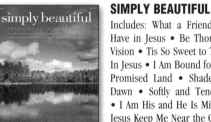

SIMPLY BEAUTIFUL

Includes: What a Friend We Have in Jesus • Be Thou My Vision • Tis So Sweet to Trust In Jesus • I Am Bound for the Promised Land • Shades of Dawn • Softly and Tenderly • I Am His and He Is Mine • Jesus Keep Me Near the Cross • Shall We Gather At the River • and many more.

_____ 35027735 Piano Solo..............................$16.95

SNOW FALLING ON IVORY

From tender carols of reflections to sparkling songs of joy, this collection has something for everybody. Includes: Dance at the Manger • Ding Dong Merrily on High • Gesu Bambino • Go, Tell It on the Mountain • In the Bleak Mid-Winter • It Came Upon a Midnight Clear • Let All Mortal Flesh Keep Silence • and more.

_____ 35020710 Piano Solo..............................$24.95

SNOW FALLING ON IVORY – VOLUME 2

Pianists may play the arrangements as piano solos or perform them in tandem with the optional instrumental descants for something truly special. Arrangers include: Joseph Martin, John Purifoy, Lee Dengler, Vicki Tucker Courtney, Brad Nix, Harry Strack, Matt Hyzer, Shirley Brendlinger, Alex-Zsolt, James Koerts and Joel Raney.

_____ 35028386 Piano Solo..............................$19.99

Shawnee Press

EXCLUSIVELY DISTRIBUTED BY

HAL•LEONARD® CORPORATION
7777 W. BLUEMOUND RD. P.O. BOX 13819 MILWAUKEE, WI 53213

Prices, contents, and availability subject to change without notice.